Butterfly Fairies

Serene creatures of myth, two butterfly fairies gently rest upon the tender stems and leaves of spring flowers. Graceful Day arises, warmed by the golden sun. And weighing little more than a moonbeam, delicate Night settles in for an evening's repose. Both magical beings are cross stitched on 28-count Antique White Monaco and custom-framed to fully capture every realistic detail.

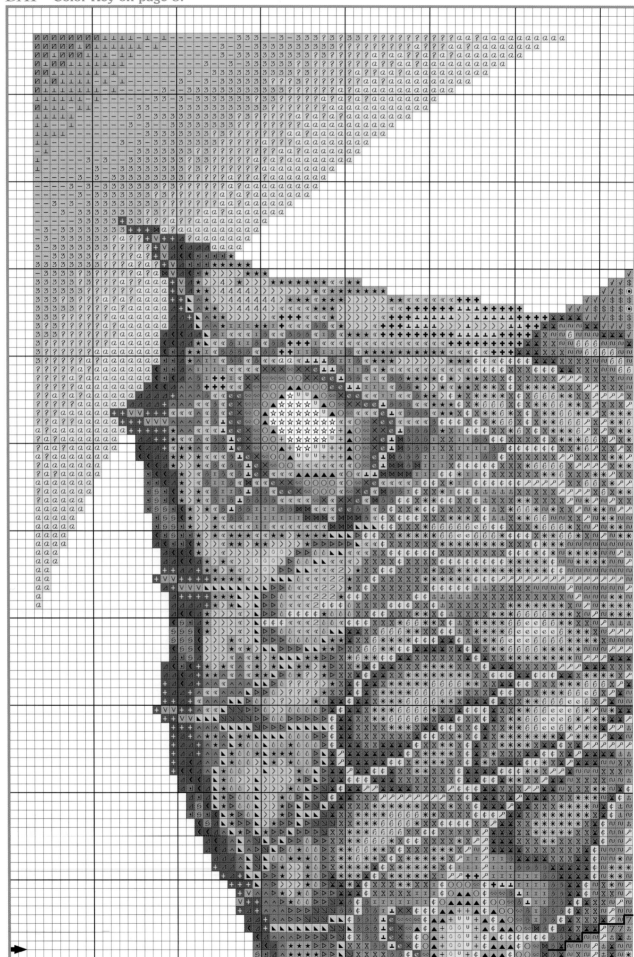

Section 2   3

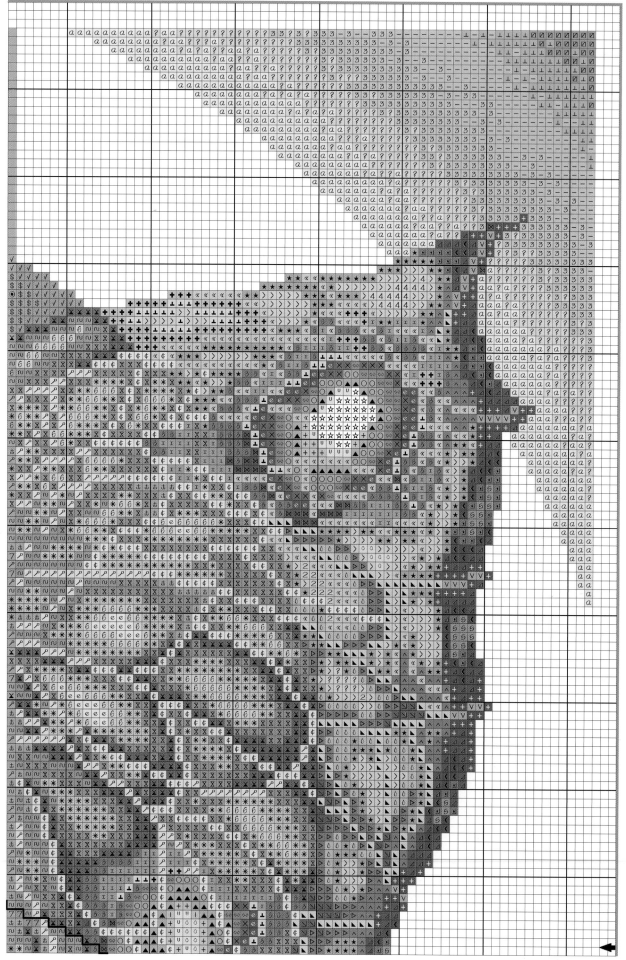

Section 3

4

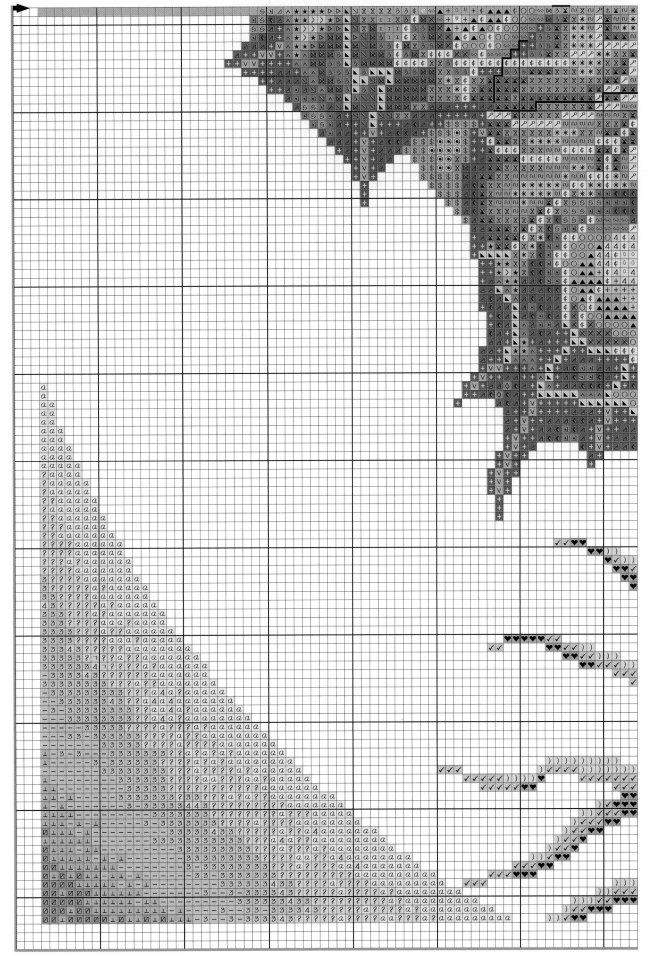

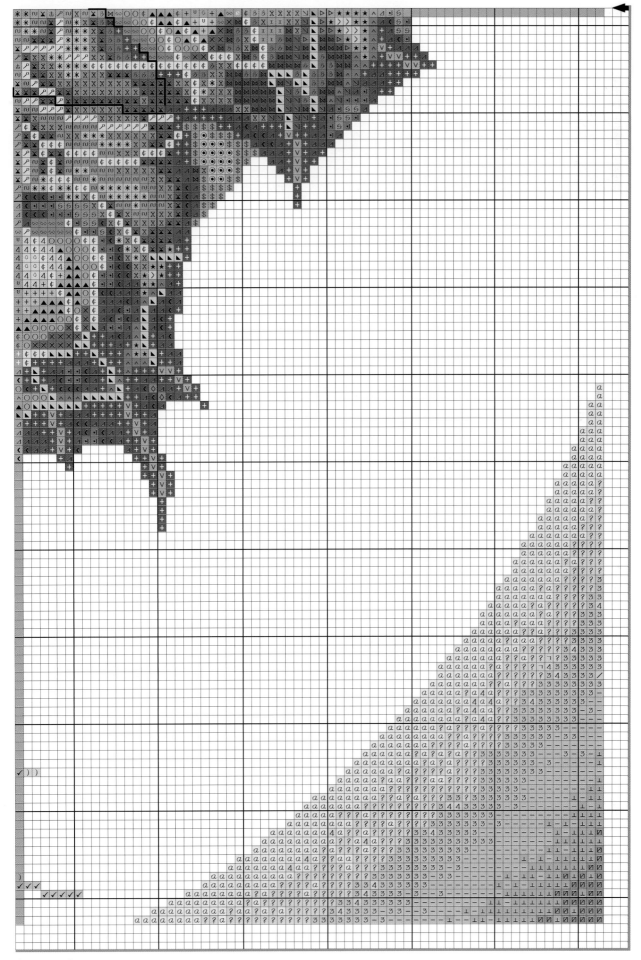

DMC	1 strand cross stitch	2 strand cross stitch	B'ST	ANC.
223		◆		895
311		✕		148
319		m		218
320		♥		215
322		∞		978
334		O		977
341		%.		117
367		c	/	217
368		✓		214
369		)		1043
422		n		943
433		◀		358
434		•|		310
435		5		1046
436	✕	◇		1045
437	~	V		362
518	▨			1039
519	⊥			1038
610	▼	N		889
611	7	▷		898
612	‡			832
613		◊		831
676		~		891
677		⬇		886
739		◣		387
744		I		301
745	6	♪		300
746		✕		275
760		◆◆		1022
761		#		1021
775	?	4		128
793		6		176
801		◢		359
818		∞		23
819		T		271
822		«		390
828	3	⌐		9159
838		⋈		1088
839		8	/	1086
840		I		1084
841		✚		1082
842		⊥		1080
930		⬆		1035
931		^		1034
932		★		1033
938		✚		381
945		C		881
951		=		1010

DMC	1 strand cross stitch	2 strand cross stitch	ANC.
3072	2		847
3325		+	129
3328		H	1024
3712		Z	1023
3713		<	1020
3721					896
3722		n	1027
3743		✳	869
3747		~	120
3750		e	1036
3752		>	1032
3755		▲	140
3756	a	0	1037
3761	−	/	928
3770		△	1009
3787	♡		273
3823	e	¢	386
3827	✕	$	311
3841		U	9159
3854		√	313
3855	✳	◉	311
3865		☆	2
B5200		♡	1

▨ Purple area indicates last row of previous section of design.

Design was stitched on a 21" x 21" piece of 28 count Antique White Monaco (design size 15" x 15") over two fabric threads. One and two strands of floss were used for Cross Stitch and one strand for Backstitch. It was custom framed.

The chart is divided into six sections. Use the following diagram for placement.

SECTION 1	SECTION 2	SECTION 3
SECTION 4	SECTION 5	SECTION 6

Stitch Count (210w x 210h)

14 count	15"	x 15"
16 count	13⅛"	x 13⅛"
18 count	11¾"	x 11¾"

DMC	1 strand cross stitch	2 strand cross stitch	B'ST	ANC.
225		7		1026
311	L	I		148
312	S	◣		979
316		◇		1017
319		0		218
322	=	<		978
334	×	◤		977
367		8		217
368		C		214
433	3	◆		358
434	▶	n		310
435	‡	‖		1046
436		□		1045
437		∩		362
500		⊥		683
501		◑		878
502		L		877
503		(		876
518		O		1039
519		▲		1038
611	⊙	√		898
612	¢	$		832
613	♥	≡		831
644	★			830
738		/		361
746	⊘	<		275
775	◇	%		128
778		+		968
801	∞	H		359
819		♡		271
828		U		9159
924	2	↑		851
926	#	√	/	850
927	6	>		848
930		▣		1035
931	⋈	m		1034
938	✳	Z		381
951		4		1010
3021	0	a		905
3041		▷		871
3042		)		870
3078		V		292
3325	⊠	T		129

DMC	1 strand cross stitch	2 strand cross stitch	B'ST	ANC.
3727		•		1016
3740		◥		873
3750		⊘		1036
3755	♦♦	✳		140
3756	↘	↑		1037
3760		−		169
3761		+		928
3768	▬	∧	/	779
3770		m		1009
3790	=	≪	/	393
3813		~		875
3816		n		876
3823	e	△		386
3841	∼	♡		9159
3860		▮		379
3861		S		378
3865	☆	◿		2

▨ Purple area indicates last row of previous section of design.

Design was stitched on a 21" x 21" piece of 28 count Antique White Monaco (design size 15" x 15") over two fabric threads. One and two strands of floss were used for Cross Stitch and one strand for Backstitch. It was custom framed.

The chart is divided into six sections. Use the following diagram for placement.

SECTION 1	SECTION 2	SECTION 3
SECTION 4	SECTION 5	SECTION 6

Stitch Count (210w x 210h)

14 count	15"	x 15"
16 count	$13^1/_8$"	x $13^1/_8$"
18 count	$11^3/_4$"	x $11^3/_4$"

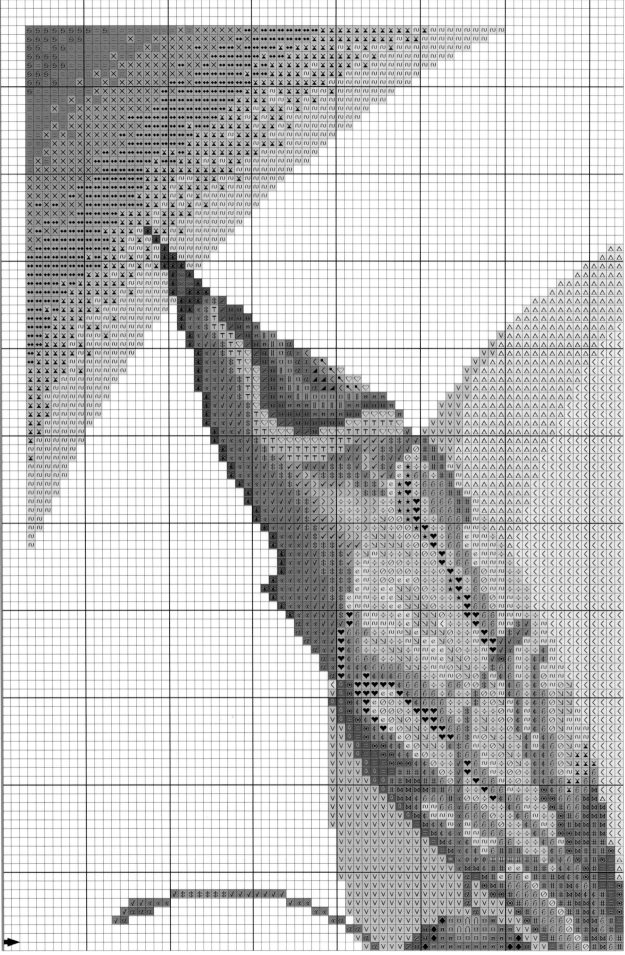

Section 1

10

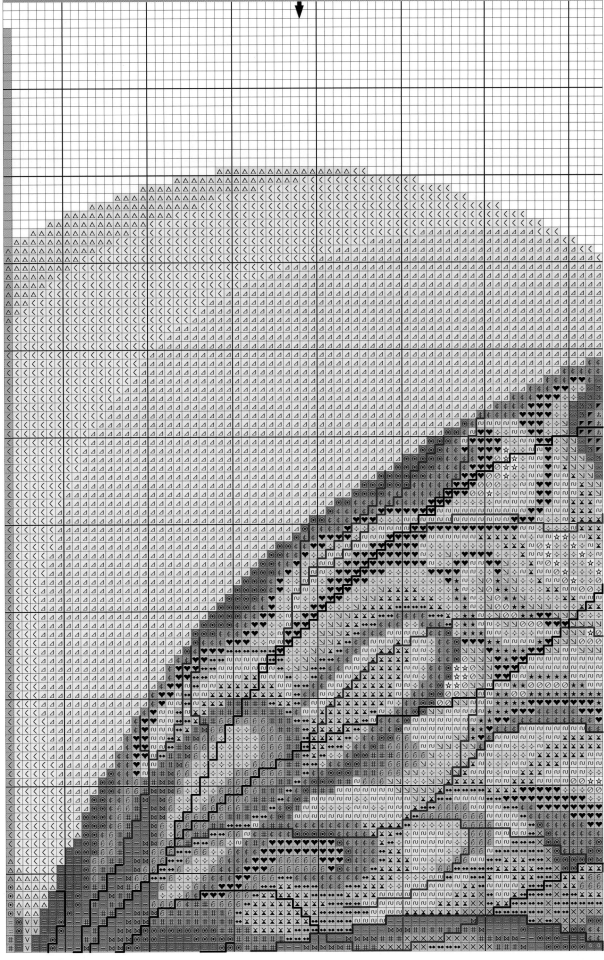

Section 2

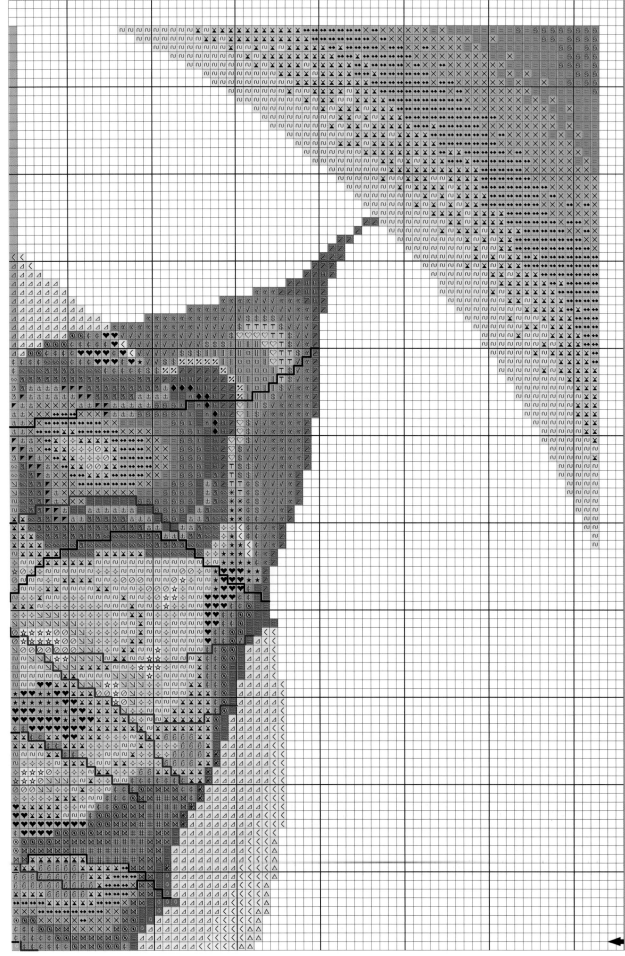

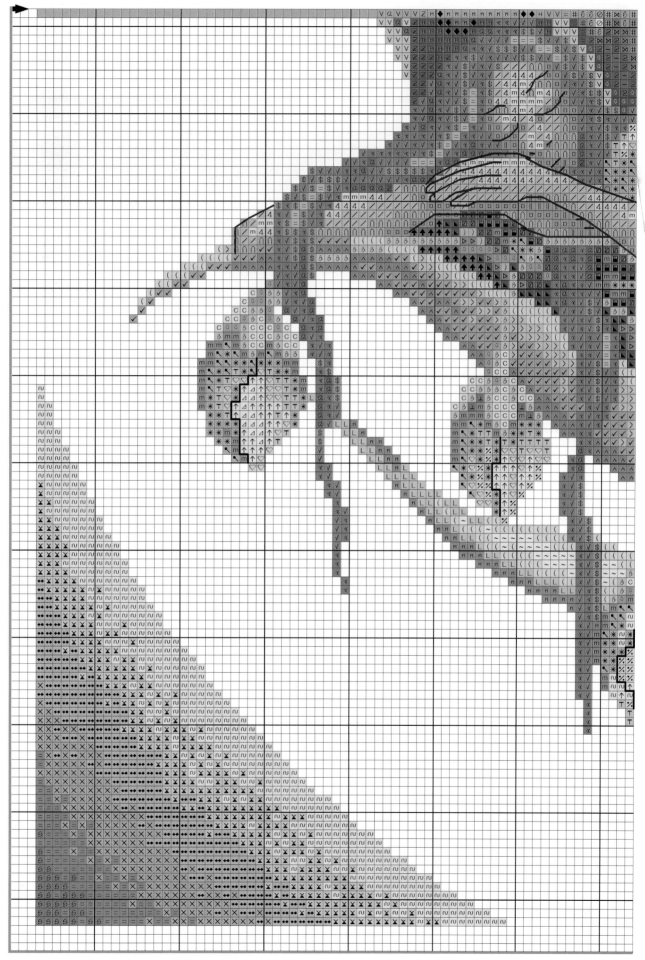

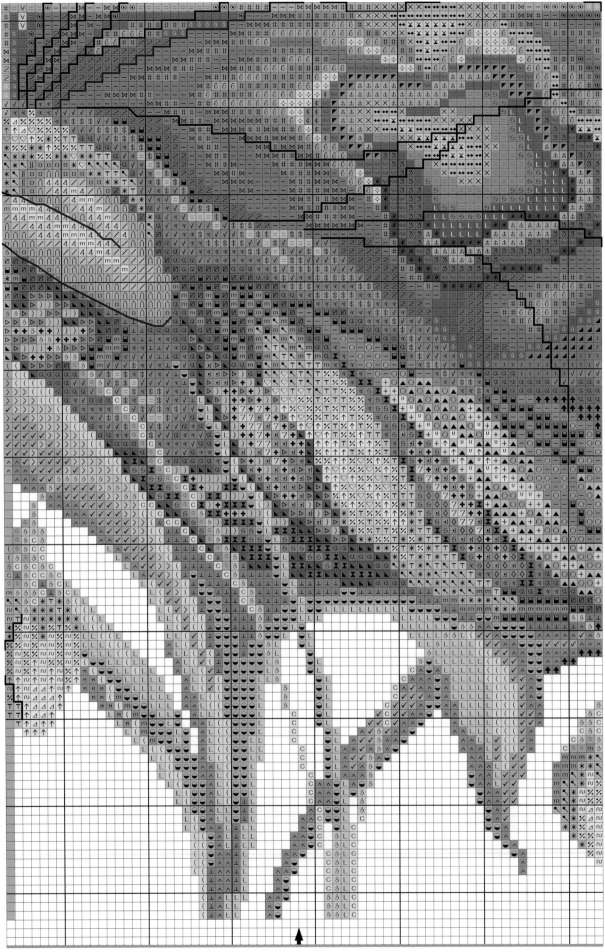

HOW TO READ CHARTS

Each chart is made up of a key and a gridded design where each square represents a stitch. The symbols in the key tell which floss color to use for each stitch in the chart. The following headings and symbols are given:

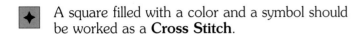

      X — Cross Stitch
      DMC — DMC color number
      B'ST — Backstitch
      ANC. — Anchor color number

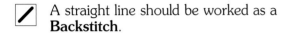

A square filled with a color and a symbol should be worked as a **Cross Stitch**.

A straight line should be worked as a **Backstitch**.

Sometimes the symbol for a **Cross Stitch** may be partially covered when a **Backstitch** crosses the square. Refer to the background color to determine the floss color.

HOW TO STITCH

Always work **Cross Stitches** first and then add the **Backstitch**.

Cross Stitch (X): For horizontal rows, work stitches in two journeys **(Fig. 1)**. For vertical rows, complete each stitch as shown **(Fig. 2)**. When working over two fabric threads, work Cross Stitch as shown in **Fig. 3**.

Fig. 1   **Fig. 2**   **Fig. 3**

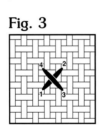

Backstitch (B'ST): For outlines and details, Backstitch should be worked after the design has been completed **(Fig. 4)**. When working over two fabric threads, work Backstitch as shown in **Fig. 5**.

Fig. 4   **Fig. 5**

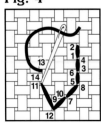
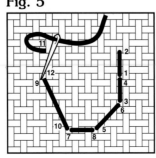

STITCHING TIPS

Dye Lot Variation

It is important to buy all of the floss you need to complete your project from the same dye lot. Although variations in color may be slight when flosses from two different dye lots are held together, the variation is usually apparent on a stitched piece.

Where to Start

The horizontal and vertical centers of each charted design are shown by arrows. You may start at any point on the charted design, but be sure the design will be centered on the fabric. Locate the center of fabric by folding in half, top to bottom and again left to right. On the charted design, count the number of squares (stitches) from the center of the chart to where you wish to start. Then from the fabric's center, find your starting point by counting out the same number of fabric threads (stitches). *(To work over two fabric threads, count out twice the number of fabric threads.)*

Working over Two Fabric Threads

When working over two fabric threads, the stitches should be placed so that vertical fabric threads support each stitch. Make sure that the first Cross Stitch is placed on the fabric with stitch 1-2 beginning and ending where a vertical fabric thread crosses over a horizontal fabric thread **(Fig. 6)**.

Fig. 6

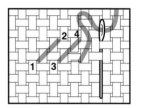

We have made every effort to ensure that these instructions are accurate and complete. We cannot, however, be responsible for human error, typographical mistakes, or variations in individual work.

Production Team: Writer – Mimi Harrington; Editorial Writer – Susan McManus Johnson; Graphic Artist – Karen F. Allbright; and Photo Stylist – Karen Hall.